Dream Along With Me

Join the Author
As He Recollects His
Most Bizarre Dreams

Joe Layton

Dream Along With Me
Copyright © 2024 by Joe Layton

All rights reserved. No part of this publication may be reproduced, distributed, or transmitted in any form or by any means, including photocopying, recording, or other electronic or mechanical methods, without the prior written permission of the author, except in the case of brief quotations embodied in critical reviews and certain other non-commercial uses permitted by copyright law.

Tellwell Talent
www.tellwell.ca

ISBN
978-1-7-7962484-0 (Paperback)
978-1-7-7962485-7 (eBook)

Dedicated to my wonderful wife Lorri who has endured yelps, screams and thrashing limbs while lying next to me in my dreamworld journeys.

TABLE OF CONTENTS

Preface vii
Introduction ix

Soaring Dreams 1
Aliens 7
This An That 11
The Seashore 19
More This An That 27
Work Related 59
Back To This An That 73

PREFACE

From an early age I can remember having very vivid dreams. Sometimes they were scary nightmares and other dreams were pleasant and enjoyable. After many years of discussing my dreams with family and friends, many of whom were amazed at my ability to recall dreams, I finally began to record my dreams in a journal at the age of 64. I have had so many interesting dreams that I decided to share a number them by recollecting them in this book. I dream in color and my most enjoyable dreams involve soaring (yes, I fly in my dreams) or body surfing. Common themes in my dreams include work (even after I retired), visiting seashore towns, and travel in general. I have had my share of sexual dreams which I have kept to myself and are not discussed in this book. I have been shot at close range (always in the stomach for some reason) and chased or otherwise accosted by wild animals. Many of my dreams include relatives, close friends or co-workers. I have changed their names in the book that follows to protect their identities.

INTRODUCTION

Everything was the color orange. Wall to wall orange. Nothing was visible except for solid orange. I knew I was in bed sleeping and knew I was about to have a nightmare. They all started the same – a field of bright orange. Then a black dot would appear in the center of the field of orange. The dot would slowly start moving in a counterclockwise direction in a spiraling fashion. As the dot moved it left a trail of black in the form of a spiral. The dot spiraled faster and faster leaving a black trail which expanded until my entire field of vision was black. Then the black disappeared and a scene came into view. I was about 4 years old and pedaling my tricycle madly down the sidewalk as a gorilla chased me. All of this served as the introduction to a nightmare. Then, a curtain would open, as if in a movie theatre, and my nightmare for that night would begin. I had these nightmares as well as other dreams for many years when I was a youngster. The nightmares gradually went away as I aged (a good thing because they were very scary – I remember being shot in the stomach with a pistol held at close range on several occasions) but the dreams continued.

One of my most vivid dreams occurred in September 2019. The dog had run out the back door at our home in rural New Jersey and down the driveway followed on his bicycle by my son. I followed, intending to tell my son to not go too far in pursuit of the dog. When I came out the door, I immediately had the sensation of heat on the right side of my neck. I looked to the right and up in the sky I saw a white-hot arrow pointing to the ground. It was throbbing and was the source of the heat. On the ground, directly below the arrow, on a hill in the forest next to our house, a group of humans or human-like figures were moving about in a circle and chanting in an unknown language.

Many of the shots to the stomach dreams occurred when I was younger, before I started my journal. However, I recently had one at the age of 77. I was on a what seemed to be a work related trip to Delaware where myself and three others were touring the countryside looking for homeowners with large displays of flowers. One in particular stood out – it was a house at the end of a narrow lane with large flower beds on either side of the driveway and on an embankment at the end of driveway next to the house. After recording the location of the house for a guidebook we were preparing we stopped at a small hall associated with either a firehouse or VFW. Inside there was a large table with four guys playing cards and drinking beer. We joined them at the other end of the table to sit and have lunch. One of the guys was very belligerent, a bully. A different guy spilled a beer on the table and the bully told me I was going to buy a newspaper from him for $20 and use it to sop up the beer. I refused. The four guys then took us to a nearby house. We were sitting in the living room of this house with me and my three companions on a sofa and opposite us was the bully sitting on a living room chair. The bully got up, pulled out a handgun, and came over to me and shot me three times in the stomach. There were two rapid bangs, a brief pause, and then a third bang. I looked down and saw I wasn't bleeding so either the gun wasn't loaded or was firing blanks. I was incensed and turned into a maniac. I grabbed the gun from the bully, pistol whipped him and threw him to the floor where I bashed his head into the floor repeatedly

SOARING DREAMS

My earliest soaring dreams occurred long before I began to keep a dream journal. In one dream I was soaring in and around a ski area that my son frequented in NY State. In another I recall jumping off my parent's house roof and proceeding to soar around the town. In a very vivid dream, I was soaring somewhere in the southern Appalachian Mountains when I soared over a ridge and on the other side was the most dramatic fall colors as leaves were at their peak color. The reds, oranges and yellows were fantastic. I was in awe!

In my journal I recorded that I took my wife on a soar to visit our friends, the Nortons. I soared like Superman (but slower) towing my wife along who was holding on to my left ankle. At one point she thought she saw Mr. Norton on the ground below but when we soared closer, we saw it wasn't him. We soared quite high over an estuary but soared back home without visiting our friends when we realized the basement windows back home were not locked (5/25/10).

I had a very vivid soaring dream some years later. I and others were jumping out of plane with snow skis on so we could land on ski slopes. We soared for 10-20 miles. At one point I got so much lift that I was bumping up against the ceiling of the sky just like the ceiling in a room. Eventually we landed but well beyond any ski slopes. It was difficult to land on the flat snowless ground with skis on and we did this by extending our legs out and flapping our arms and using tree branches to break our fall (11/12/14).

The following year I once again gave my wife a soaring ride. I had my arms outstretched in the soaring position with my wife laying on top of them perpendicular to my body. I leaped off the roof of a house and soared around it twice and I decided to loop around it four more times but I couldn't do it and had to land on the ground after 3 1/2 loops (8/30/15).

I went several years without recording a dream, but I don't think I missed any soaring dreams. Those were usually vivid or at least "cool" and worthy of recording. On this particular night, or early morning (6 AM) I dreamt that by filling my lungs with air and holding my breath I was able to float and move about by kicking my legs and stroking my arms much like I was swimming. I was floating (flying) down the streets passing up and over telephone and electric wires strung between poles. After flying around a bit I inspected the roof of my house by floating above it as neighbors watched from below (11/23/19).

I was working at XYZ Consulting, and we had moved into two new office buildings on the east shores of a lake that had flooded. After a week the flood waters still had not receded. A road went around the lake and the rear building was only accessible because of the flood waters by driving around the far side (west side) of the lake. I drove around the west side of the lake to access the building in the rear. The water level was slightly above the first-floor elevation in this building. I met some XYZ employees who worked in the survey department and told them I was going to check out the other building. They pointed out that the road was flooded and impassable between the two buildings. Much to their amazement I said I would fly over to the other building. I gulped several deep breaths of air and floated over to the other building which was about ¼ mile away. I started to lose altitude about ¾ of the way to the second building, but I regained it by gulping more air and flapping my arms. I ascended to about 200 feet above ground and then glided to a landing at the second building. There were a number of people from various firms at this building as the flood waters were below the first floor and it was accessible from the main road. The XYZ offices were on the upper floors and an ID was required as well as passing through an obstacle course to get in. First up on the obstacle course it was required to climb a ladder which led to a platform on which there was a horizontal fan turning. You had to step between the fan blades as they turned. Fortunately for me a woman stepped between the blades and stood there stopping the blades from rotating with her legs. Next, I had to straddle a steel beam and scoot across an opening 20 feet long which was about 50 feet above the floor below. Next, I had to crawl through something similar to an air conditioning duct for about 75 feet. It was a tight fit and I had to lay prone and pull my body along with the fingertips. Upon emerging I was directed down a hallway to XYZ offices where I was greeted by an accounting department employee named Nicole Kidman. I told her I recognized her name. We proceeded into the accounting department office which was bright white with gold accents. The desks were made out of clouds. I asked for directions to the rest of the office and went down a hallway where I came across a room which was apparently a breakroom for disabled employees or employees who tired easily. There were about 8 naked employees in this room all lying on the floor. There was a male about 7 feet tall stretched out to his full length and a female about 3-4 feet tall curled up in a fetal position. I never found the rest of the office and as the dream came to an end I regretted not having the opportunity to fly back to the other building and entertain questions about how I was able to fly (4/7/22).

ALIENS

In a dream I cast a fishing line up into the sky and caught a small alien when he became entangled in the line. The alien in turn spun a sticky web around himself and the line and attempted to snare me in the web. I avoided the sticky web and moved away and was not too concerned as the alien was only the size of a baseball (6/8/10).

The aliens returned to my dreams nearly 12 years later. I was in a large bowl trapped under an alien spaceship shaped like a hot air balloon but without an opening in the bottom or an attached basket. I was being sucked up the side of the balloon between the balloon and wall of the bowl. At one point I started to get sucked inside the balloon and I reached out and grabbed something which stopped me from being sucked in. I then slid down the side of the bowl and found I was holding a stair railing in one hand and a step attached to a balustrade in the other hand. Ther were other humans at the bottom of the bowl who cheered since I had escaped being sucked into the balloon (2/19/22).

I arrived on the planet Uranus. Not sure how I got there but it appeared I had caught the wrong bus. I was standing on a street corner trying to converse with a Uranus native who was very human-like. Indeed, Uranus looked very much like earth from what I could see. I was trying to describe to this Uranian where I came from and was pointing to the sky but he didn't respond (2/24/21).

Aliens apparently had arrived in eastern Pennsylvania. They captured an adult male and had wrapped him in rubber (similar to the rubber from which car tires are made) and set the rubber on fire. The rubber and guy burnt up as he screamed. The aliens took refuge in a vehicle that was similar to a trojan horse. It was made of a metal-like substance and was gray in color with purple spots randomly arranged on the surface. A military fighter jet strafed it with machine gun fire but the bullets just bounced off. I had observed this on the TV but since the activity was only about 50 miles from my location I began to panic and proceeded to close all the windows and draw the blinds in the house. Later I was apparently chosen to help fight the aliens and was told it was necessary to become more energetic and powerful. This was to be accomplished by attaching two power packs to my body. The first step was to drive nails into my chest and abdomen to see if they would stick and provide support to the power packs. The nails held and the power packs were fastened; one on my chest and the other on my abdomen. Then channels about ½ inch deep and ½ inch wide were cut across my chest and abdomen and wires attached to the power packs were laid in the channels and I was sewn up. Fortunately, I woke before I had to face the aliens (10/1/24).

THIS AN THAT

I was at a new acquaintance's house in a faraway place. I let a 6'10" tall stranger into the house who proceeded to talk about a computer model to predict downstream traffic flow. I listened to his presentation and then he suddenly pulled a handgun out and shot me in the stomach, neck and shoulders. I didn't feel a thing and I awoke thinking it must have been a fake gun (7/20/10).

I was on a tour of Ohio cities with a senior citizens group. I was with my mom and also with us was my wife and twin sons. Around Noon we stopped at a house so the seniors could listen to a favorite radio show. We were touring Dayton and walked past a stadium and then down a main street lined with sub shops. One shop had a chain-driven conveyor belt which exited the second floor of the building and continued outside for about 6 feet before reentering the building. The conveyor belt was carrying large imitation sub rolls – it was apparently an advertising gimmick. We stopped in a shop and were greeted by a man of middle eastern descent wearing a fan shaped hat (like an upright visor) that had the menu on it in a foreign language. All of a sudden, my mother began speaking to him in his native language (the only word I could understand was Brooklyn). Apparently, this man was from Brooklyn and my mother had figured it out. I never heard my mother speak this language outside of this dream (8/7/10).

I was with God who turns out to be a marketing genius. In the dream he came up with ideas for new recreational items like ski doos or wave runners with unique shapes (like fighter jets) and vivid colors (deep blue, lime green). All designs were instant hits (10/14/10).

I was driving with my wife in a hilly area somewhere on the east coast. It was snowing in some locations but not in others. We continued driving and a half day later we were in California. Our destination was to pick up our daughter who was in pre-school. We drove through an attractive town which had a little of everything – stores, restaurants, theatres, offices, etc. and eventually drove up a long hill that was developed with suburban housing. Driving up the hill we had a birds-eye perspective of the town. Before picking up our daughter we stopped at a breeder of turkey dogs-a cross between a turkey and a dog. They had four legs and fur, not feathers. My wife had ordered two of these dogs as pets without my knowledge and we were picking them up (11/14/10).

I decided to hold a fundraiser for a charity that was not apparent in this dream. I determined an attraction that could raise funds was a ride in a cigarette hulled open ocean racing boat. To get a sponsor I pulled the name Mull off the office building where I worked. I knew nothing about this business and had never met anyone who worked there but nevertheless decided to name them the sponsor. The rest of the dream was spent trying to contact the Mull people to let them know they were the sponsor, arranging for the boat and conducting fundraising activities (3/30/10).

I was jogging for an extremely long time without tiring. I was barefoot and transitioned from jogging to doing wind sprints along Bannard Street in Freehold. I was in a costume (Santa Claus?) and stopped in a small crafts shop at the end of the street to pick up something for my wife. I waited for the proprietor who turned out to be a realtor from our hometown. The realtor was also in costume (4/1/10).

I was walking eastbound on Route 522 (Throckmorton Street) past the St. Rose cemetery in Freehold with my sisters. We saw a female tiger with several cubs to our left. Someone said to watch out because the male tiger is probably nearby. Suddenly a male tiger leaped out of some bushes along the road (4/3/10).

Following the above dream, I stayed with an acquaintance, Ed at a rustic cabin in the woods. His wife came home in a VW beetle and jumped out of the car naked and soaking wet with a towel over one shoulder. My guess was she was returning from the gym after a workout and quick shower. She cast me a glance as she ambled into the house and I said "good thing you weren't in an accident ". Ed seemed to take offense to this (4/3/1).

Was fishing in a rowboat with my wife who caught a big largemouth bass which appeared to be over 5 lbs. When we went to weigh it, however, we found our fish scale limit was only 2 ½ lbs. (4/15/10).

My two sons and myself were preparing to decorate an evergreen tree for Christmas at the end of our driveway. We had large lights in the shape of angels. As we untangled the light strings about 25 feet from the tree two girls, maybe 5 or 6 years old, came up to the tree and broke off the lower center branch, ruining the tree's proportions. The dream ended as me and the boys were deciding whether or not it was even worthwhile to continue decorating the tree (8/21/10).

I was loaned a white British sports car by a woman whose friend owned the car. I drove the car around a bit but when I returned it to the woman who had loaned it to me it had turned into an inflatable bike that had lost air and gone limp and had to be inflated (8/25/10).

One of my sons and other neighborhood kids were playing in a cornfield which was only 10 feet wide and extended alongside and in front of our house. They found a small football shaped object that turned out to be a trigger mechanism for a bomb (9/22/10).

I was in a long line of cars at three ATM machines. When I pulled up to the ATM in my line the cover came off. I got out of the car and put the cover aside so I could access the keypad which was hanging by a wire. No matter how hard I tried I couldn't get it to work much to the chagrin of drivers in line behind me who were growing inpatient (9/22/10).

I was commuting to work in an RV. In order to get better gas mileage there were pedals mounted inside much like a paddle boat. I would pedal back and forth to work to save money on gas with the added advantage of losing weight (2/5/12).

Lots of dreams in early February of 2012. A brief summary:

My wife and I walked our bikes along drainage ditches in Florida. The paths were very overgrown with weeds making them difficult to traverse.

My wife and I at an awards ceremony at Rutgers – both of us were sized for blazers, similar to Masters Golf Tournament, beforehand and blazers were given to us emblematic of this reward (what the award was for I have no clue).

My wife and I were at a wedding in Chevy Chase, Maryland. We met our friends Rachel and Dick after the ceremony and left with their very nice SUV leaving our SUV behind as our friends were flying off on a trip.

February 28th was memorable for the dreams I seemingly had nonstop all night long. There was a dream where I was an overnight watchman stationed at a gatehouse next to a NJ Transit railroad crossing. Another dream involved filling out qualifications forms at work (a task I was doing in real life at the time.). The longest dream involved driving toward Washington NJ where I used to live and being passed on the road by my handy neighbor Mike from Basking Ridge where I lived after Washington. I followed Mike and he turned into the street where I used to live. I thought he might be there to do some handyman work at the home for autistic adults across from my former home where repairs of some sort always seemed to be needed. I chatted with Mike about the autistic house after we got out of our cars on the street. After a while he said "You know I am not Mike ". And he wasn't; but the guy in the car who passed me in his car and turned into my street certainly was. I walked across the street to my old home and there on a blanket sat my adult daughter with a female cousin from Boston. My daughter had just had a baby girl but the baby was not with her. The cousin had a baby boy with her whose body was about 80% penis. The baby coughed violently and spit out phlegm. The yard was eroded with small gullies created by water flowing from multiple pipes that were draining from the house. After this lenghy dream I had the following dream.

I have avoided posting my erotic dreams here since they are numerous and mostly not of interest to others. One I have to report however, involved foreplay with my wife followed by me lying on my back and ejaculating. This is of note since my prostate was removed in December 2010 making ejaculation impossible. I lay there in my dream thinking a miracle had just occurred. Everything was so realistic that when I woke, I had to check myself only to find my pajamas were dry. No miracles tonight (2/28/12).

THE SEASHORE

I visited Massachusetts by myself except I brought Bongo, my dog along. I dropped Bongo off at a canine amusement park along the coast so he could entertain himself. I proceeded South and met my uncles Jim and Chuck and cousin Mal (all of whom had passed on well before this dream). We were along the coast and Jim said the tidal current was very strong between our location and the amusement park where Bongo was, and he suggested to Mal that he swim up to get Bongo even though it was several miles away. Mal thought this was a cool idea, so he jumped into the water – end of dream (1/29/11).

Continuing with the amusement park theme, I was at an amusement park (for people) somewhere in the South. I put on little self-propelled hovercraft devices, one on each foot, and cruised around a lake. Later I took a bus trip to view Southern mansions and plantations (2/2/11).

Bongo our dog appeared in several dreams before the Massachusetts dream. I dreamt I met a lady who owned a pet food company. The companies' bags were red with a dog's image that looked a lot like Bongo. Because of this resemblance I gave Bongo away to this lady (4/18/10).

My seashore dreams include the first one I recorded in my journal. I was swimming in Old Orchard Beach, Maine late in the summer season and the water was very warm for Maine. The tide was very strong, and the downtown area did not look like I remembered from an actual visit years before. After my swim I drove back nonstop to N.J. and went to my office. Once there I discovered I could not recall my password to retrieve voicemail. I was desperately trying to recall my password when I woke up (3/28/10).

A week later my dreams took me to Acadia National Park in Maine. I marveled at the surf crashing against the shoreline rocks. I came across a long incline of a rock formation that led to the water and was mostly smooth. I took a chair (actually the chair I used at one communities municipal Zoning Board meetings) and discovered that I could slide very fast down the incline while sitting in the chair. I did this several times and afterward walked through a shower spray that was in the form of an elongated arch (4/7/10).

I was in a tropical environment with a barrier island seperating the ocean from a bay. The odd thing was the water level in the ocean was at least 10 feet higher than the water level in the bay. While trying to figure out why this was so I moved onto a second dream that I didn't recall at all (5/1/10).

Moving on to the West Coast my son and I went to a Pacific Ocean beach to observe what we thought would be a heavy surf. As it turns out the water level was high but no real surf. We walked along the beach and came upon a cove which was very beautiful. There were shops along the oceanfront and the water level was close to the front doors of the shops but the water, fortunately, was calm. Beyond the cove there was a massage parlor and my wife joined me while my son disappeared. Good thing because my wife proceeded to receive a "sexual stimulation" massage from an older female while I watched and held her hand (5/11/11). After this dream I had no entries in my journal until February 2012.

In my second dream of the night I was visiting a tropical Island, most likely Hawaii. I was traveling with a tour group without my family, so I guess I was single. There were towering cliffs rising above ocean inlets. Occasionally tremendous waves that reached up to 100 feet high on the cliffs would crash ashore soaking everything. I climbed down the cliffs to a small sandy shore and observed the water teeming with life with large creatures swimming close to shore and catching smaller fish in the shallows. My dreams are mostly in color, but this one was very colorful. I woke but fell back asleep into the same dream; something I do frequently (2/12/12).

In one of five dreams I had in one night me and my son were walking on the shoreline of Raritan Bay and there were a number of small inlets, each with it's own hand operated drawbridge. When the tide went out, we could see each inlet had very steep sides about 30 feet high. My son was jumping off the top of the inlet cliffs into the water and then climbing back up the nearly vertical cliffs (2/17/12).

I experienced what I recorded as a cool and colorful dream around 5 AM. Many of my most vivid dreams occur between 5 and 7 AM. My family had rented a small speedboat for an aquatic tour of a portion of Italy where there were a number of scenic protected bays. At one point I was by myself when I passed a beach with a big shaggy and dirty white dog with three equally shaggy and dirty pups. I then met up with my wife and her friend Lydia in a nearby village where we stopped at a small café to grab a bite. Later we were joined by the whole family and we went on a long boat tour past a refinery and then into more open waters where it got a little dicey with waves. We reentered calmer waters and cruised along the shoreline where we came upon hundreds of small octopi in the water. We then noticed small sheds along the shoreline with their ends open to the water. The sheds were lined with shelves with octopi on each shelf. Smaller octopi were on the lower shelves and the top shelf had very large octopi. The larger octopi were very colorful with red, blue and black spots (12/5/12).

At a seashore with high cliffs again! I was at a restaurant on top of the cliff looking out over the ocean. The restaurant looked like the Guggenheim Museum with circular terraces wrapping around the building and down the cliff. A friend and I decided to pole vault in reverse down the terraces. We would lean over and place a pole vaulter's pole on the terrace below and spring down and over the terrace below to the one below that. It was very tricky but we made it to the bottom (1/21/14).

Two quick seashore dreams in one night. In first I was with my wife walking along shoreline and there were humongous waves crashing on rock formations just offshore. In the second, my daughter was with me but she was very young. I had the good fortune to have my snow skis with me despite the fact we were staying at an oceanfront hotel in a tropical area. Fortunate to have the skis since I was able to ski down a steep part of the beach when there was an unexpected 8 inch snowfall. Inexplicably, people were on the beach in their swimsuits while I skied in the snow (3/20/20).

I was in the Boston area having been recruited to study the effects of waves from an impending "Northeaster". The storm produced a lot of wind but very little precipitation as it was well offshore. As the storm passed, I went down to an enclosed bay surrounded by hills on the shore and got onto a small boat. The water in the bay was very calm without even a ripple and you could see down 15-20 feet in the water. I jumped in the water and swam around a bit. Got back in the boat and went to the mouth of the bay where it joined the ocean. There was a fishing cabin at the end of a point extending into the ocean. Here the waves were crashing around the cabin to such an extent that foam was dripping off the roof of the cabin. The cabin was designed with wooden slats for a floor so that water that entered from wave action ran off between the slats and back to the ocean. There was a breakwater that ran off to the left at a 45-degree angle to the shore. The incoming waves would crash over the breakwater and reform before entering a bowl-shaped area surrounded by rocks. The waves would then explode against the rocks sending foam and water over the cabin. Despite the waves I saw 4 or 5 boats with guys fishing just offshore. The boats would ride up each wave crest and down the other side. There was also a fisherman in a canoe close to shore who was reeling in a fish. Then, suddenly Ted Williams appeared outside the fishing cabin which was apparently his. He said conditions were great for catching fish and he made a cast from alongside the cabin and instantly reeled in a fish about 2 feet long. When he got the fish ashore on the rocks he asked if I would take the fish off the hook – which I did. End of dream (11/10/21).

My wife and I were on a beach on a tropical island, and I was psyched to do some bodysurfing. Daylight Savings Time had not come yet and it was already getting dark at 4:30 P.M. Occasionally there was a very large wave. I swam out about a ½ mile and caught a huge wave that had to be about 30 feet tall and rode it all the way to the beach (4/7/22).

Once again I was visiting a New England seashore town. A river coursed through town on its way to the ocean. The river was lined with residences, shops and restaurants. There was also an indoor ice-skating rink and I had brought along my skates. I stayed at a house along the river with my Massachusetts cousins. In the morning I swam down the river and out to the ocean, with my ice skates in tow, where I did some bodysurfing. After a series of large waves that I surfed it appeared as if no more large waves were on the horizon and I told those near me I was going in. After reaching the shore a rogue wave crashed on the boardwalk injuring some people. I then walked up a street parallel to the river hoping to get back to a boardwalk on the riverbanks. However, the street was lined with shops and residences which butted up against each other blocking access between the street and river. I tried walking on the street with my skates on but the street surface was too hard. I asked passerby if there was a passage to the river explaining that at least I could walk on the boardwalk with my skates on. Someone showed me an alley connecting to the river at which point I woke up (5/1/22).

MORE THIS AN THAT

We were in the process of moving our business office to a new location when several co-workers and I went out for a walk at lunch. We walked down a series of short blocks at a pace that enabled us to cross each intersection just as the traffic light turned amber. Then we crossed an intersection as the traffic light turned red. A jaywalking trap had been set up by the police and I was pulled aside and asked to produce my driver's license which had expired. The police were making a big to do about the expired license and I asked what the license had to do with walking. They announced they were going to arrest me because the license was not only expired but it did not have my name on it but instead had the name of a convicted felon (2/6/11).

Was in the audience at an amphitheater on a college campus. The presenters of the program collected money from all attendees asking them to "empty their pockets". The presenters then announced that one lucky individual in the audience would win all the cash collected. The cash was stored in large plastic jars (like UTZ pretzel jars) on stage. The winning individual was selected by aiming an infrared pistol into the audience. I became aware that the infrared dot was locked on my forehead. This was followed shortly by a beam of liquid which gently hit me in the forehead leaving a pink dot the size of a dime marking me as the winner. I did not take home the winnings immediately because there was a lot of change in those jars and they were very heavy. I came back the next morning to claim my winnings only to discover the amphitheater was gone and was replaced by a beach. There was no sign of the money. I woke up in a panic thinking I had to find the money (2/16/11).

I dreamt my father was abusive to me and my mother; not sexually but by bullying us and using physical force. It got to the point where I killed him by ramming his head into a door jamb. I then told my mother everything was now OK (2/18/11).

In real life my father was not abusive and other dreams in which he appeared were pleasant. In one I was driving from Aberdeen Township to Freehold when I came across a barbershop that I frequented years ago. It was not too busy, so I stopped in. My dad was waiting for a haircut and my mom and two of my sisters were off to the side with shopping bags from a shopping trip. I said hello to everyone and then curled up on a couch and fell asleep. When I woke up my family was gone, and I climbed into the barber chair. I asked if my father had gotten his haircut and the barber said he did; adding that he didn't really need one. I recall that in real life my dad would get a haircut every three weeks whether he needed one or not.

The second dream of this night (this one after 6 AM) also involved my dad. Two sons and I were picking up sticks at Monmouth Avenue. My family lived there briefly when I was an infant fifty years before my sons were born; it was the home of my paternal grandfather and grandmother. My dad was with us and after picking up sticks we went with him to a luncheon at the American Legion Hall. The luncheon included an auction of artifacts that we paid little attention to until they brought out a tall 10-12-foot-tall shelving unit made of red glass. My interest was piqued by the top shelf which had a Boston Red Sox logo embossed on it. The unit was removed after a short time on the auction floor, and I went to a back room where it had been moved and inquired about its availability. I was told it was no longer available since someone offered to pay $500 for it even though the suggested value was only $46. As we prepared to leave my dad asked if we could give a friend of his a ride home. We said sure and it turned out the friend lived in the town where we did at the time. The friend lived at the far end of Mine Hill Road. Halfway to the friend's house there was a major ski area being constructed with both natural and artificial hills. We had to stop the car, get out, and pass through turnstiles. My dad's friend refused to go through the turnstiles saying he had the right to pass freely since he lived on the other side. Me, and my sons were allowed to pass through but my dad and his friend stayed behind arguing. There were hundreds of people around and the three of us went about 200 feet down the hill from the turnstiles where we could still hear my dad and his friend arguing. After about 20 minutes me and the boys went back up the hill to the turnstiles but neither my dad nor his friend were there. We asked about them and someone told us one of the two men had a heart attack and had died. I asked which one and asked if it was the bald one? Someone said they thought it was the other one but was not sure. I asked where I could find out and I was directed to several different construction sites. This was very heavy construction with steel girders holding up artificial ski hills. I approached some workers and said I needed to see the President of this operation to find out who died. I was told to wait where I was and after a while a man dragging a sack came up to me. It was obvious that the sack had a body inside. I looked in the sack but all I could see was the back of a man's head but it wasn't my dad's head, it was his friend. I asked the man if he was the

President and he said no – he was an Associate President. I complained that someone's death on site warranted the attention of the President. I was then sent to another location where I slid down a steep plywood slope that I was told was going to become a ski slope. I was still trying to find out about my dad. Finally, I was escorted to a room with a meeting table inside and several people dressed as cartoon characters joined me. Apparently, the ski slopes were going to have a cartoon theme. They tried to console me, particularly the guy to my left who was dressed in bib coveralls. A large sheet cake was brought into the room as if this would calm me down. I asked the guy to my left who he was and he said "Ray – the elf ". All I could think of as the dream came to an end was I asked to see the President to find out about my Dad and they send me Ray the elf (7/26/14).

My Dad was driving a car with my mom in the front seat and me and my wife in the back. We were traveling through Bridgewater, N.J. so I assume my parents had picked my wife and I up at our house in Basking Ridge. Our destination was my dad's sister's house in North Plainfield, N.J. I asked my Dad if he knew how to get there from where we were and he said Stelton Road. I said that may no longer be the best route because since I was a kid and we traveled there Routes I-287 and I-78 had been built (2/12/20). As an aside I have fond memories of traveling to North Plainfield during the Christmas season and seeing all the holiday lights as well as the large department stores in downtown Plainfield which we always passed through.

My Dad surprised me with a case of decent beer and a season ticket to Rutgers football. The ticket came in the form of two keys. Apparently, you needed the keys to gain access to the stadium. The beer was intended for a class I was going to take on modifying beer. Each bottle of beer was wrapped together with a can of lemon juice (1/9/21).

I went to a Rutgers football pep rally on campus at an amphitheater enclosed in a clear plastic bubble between two older buildings. I invited a date who I had never dated before and was not sure if she knew anything about football or had any interest in football. Staff shot items into the crowd from the stage. I caught a football and a canvas bag. The bag had an electronic noise maker in it. It was strange that neither the coaches nor any players appeared at the rally (2/20/11).

I went over a month without a vivid dream when I had a long one. I dreamt I was driving on Route 46 westbound near Rockaway Mall when I decided to stop at the mall which didn't look like Rockaway Mall at all. Despite the fact it was 10AM on a weekday the mall was jammed with people. I asked someone what was going on and they said "Don't you know - the President is coming ". I saw a lot of Republicans from Warren County in the crowd and despite the fact I couldn't remember who the President was I surmised he was a Republican. I got on an elevator and my roommate, George, from college was on it. I hadn't seen him for about 40 years. He was with a number of co-workers, but he was clearly their boss. I had a drink with George at a bar. He had a coke saying he was saving the hard stuff until just before he left. I had Jack Daniels on the rocks. I decided to leave and not wait for the President, and I exited the rear of the mall and walked across a field toward a road where I intended to double-back and find my car in the parking garage. When I reached the road, I heard a train whistle and saw a blue train with the Presidential Seal pull into a train station about two blocks away. I had my 35 mm single lens camera and hustled toward the train station and as I arrived I saw two large armored all-terrain vehicles with the Presidential Sea pulling away. The President had already been whisked away. As I was trying to take pictures of the train over a wall a man with a young boy asked me how much he would have to spend to purchase a camera like mine. I responded $800 to $ 1,000 and promptly woke up (4/5/11).

I joined a group for a walk along the Musconetcong River sponsored by a watershed group but I soon abandoned the group to attend church in the parish where I grew up with my wife and sons. We sat in the balcony in front of the organist. At the end of the mass an older man at the front of the balcony had his feet washed. He had a Roman type robe on and a steel cap that was of a very intricate design and he was lying in what appeared to be a small coffin. After his feet were washed he rose up from his lying position and announced it wasn't the best feet washing – he had experienced better washing of the feet in other parishes (5/26/10).

I had a car that had no body – only tubing, a seat, wheels and engine. It was white and elongated like a road grader. A skeleton of a car (6/12/10).

I ordered three things I really wanted from eBay or Craigs List. One was an Austin Healey Sprite (my first car), the second was a pair of K-2 downhill skis (my first new skis that were not second hand) and the third item I couldn't recall. The car was fine, but the skis had holes in them. One ski had a large hole right where the binding would go making it impossible to attach bindings (7/5/10).

I was playing basketball at the playground of a large high school in Philadephia. My longtime friend from

Philadelphia was in the dream. The ball went over the high fence surrounding the playground and I went to retrieve it. When I retieved the ball from the adjacent street I could not get back into the playground. I tried walking around to the front of the school and walking through the school as well as other paths but all ways were to no avail and I was not able to get back to the playground (8/5/10).

I didn't keep up with entering dreams in my journal probably because I was distracted by being diagnosed with prostate cancer in the Fall of 2010 and eventually having a radical prostatectomy in December 2010. A few dreams were recorded in 2011 and are related elsewhere in this book. I picked up again in February 2012.

I was visiting a camping area where there was a canal. Some fishing buddies and I were watching a fishing lure demonstration. Afterwards I bought a lure for $250 intended to attract a fish species I had never fished for. I was feeling foolish about spending so much money until I discovered six additional lures enclosed in the package as a bonus. We then hurried back to our campsite to prepare for running in a marathon even though none of us had ever run a marathon before (2/3/12).

I was helping a friend and fishing buddy in my town clean up his yard. He had a woodchipper that could fly like a helicopter. Another mutual friend who lived nearby came over with a buddy of his and took off in the wood chipper and flew around the neighborhood while my friend and I watched from the ground (3/26/12).

I was driving with my wife and one son, who was about 5 years old at the time, heading west on Route 57 between Washington and Phillipsburg when I saw a commercial passenger plane flying east close to the ground near Pohatcong Creek. The plane was making a noise like the engines were straining when it suddenly shot upwards and started to make a loop. I said "Wow, I didn't think a plane that big could do that ". It completed the loop having gone upside down at the top of the loop and crashed at high velocity, nose down, straight into the ground followed by a large ball of fire. I suggested we go to the site of the crash to see if there were any survivors, but my wife said it would traumatize our son and we should continue driving. I drove on thinking it was unlikely there were any survivors but if there were others would be able to help (11/27/12).

My wife and I had to walk through knee-deep snow to reach a vacant Victorian house that we wanted to explore. There were some real treasures in the house that I would have loved to take with me, but I did not. The most memorable treasures were large metal signs in a bar area that was fully stocked with liquor and shelves of glasses, each glass with a unique inscription. We left empty-handed walking back out to the street through knee-deep snow (12/3/12).

I went to a minor league baseball game at a tacky stadium in Old Bridge. I was by myself and only wanted one ticket, but the policy was a minimum of 4 so I had to buy 4 tickets. I wanted to buy some food, but the only item left at the concession stand was grilled cheese despite the fact the game had yet to start. So, I ordered a grilled cheese sandwich. The only appliance available to grill the sandwich was a toaster oven whose door would not close. The food preparer put the sandwich in the oven and walked away without turning it on. He did this twice. I was getting frustrated, so I told the preparer I was going to find my seat and then return for my sandwich. I found my seat, which was actually an aluminum folding beach chair at the end of a row. After about 5 minutes a man came along and said I was sitting in his seat. I didn't argue but instead went to get my sandwich, which of course wasn't grilled. They gave it to me anyhow but I threw it away over the stands and into nearby woods. I went back into the stands to look for my seats, but the numbering of the sections and rows made no sense. I never did find them but since the stands were ½ empty I sat wherever I could find a seat (2/21/13).

I dreamt I was part of a focus group led by our church pastor. We took a break, and I picked up a newspaper and read an article about a canoeist being very upset with the design of a passage along the Rahway River through a large embankment for either a railroad or highway. The article referred to the passage design as "ducting" which was very appropriate since a photo showed what appeared to be a large HVAC duct going through the embankment. Another photo showed a woman in a canoe entering the duct and leaning backwards almost on her back to get enough clearance to pass through. The front of the canoe entered the duct, but the woman's chest hit the top of the duct and she got stuck. A member of the focus group mentioned to me he heard of this problem and how it was poor planning on the part of the designers who promised a passageway through the embankment that made it possible for canoeists to go from one side to the other without leaving their canoes. The focus group reconvened and I woke up (3/5/13).

The family went to a Rutgers Football game against a Division II college just across the Delaware River. We stayed in a college dorm overnight since it was late summer, and school was not yet in session. We ran with the team and cheered them on as they ran through city streets and then cut through a field next to the stadium. After the game we went back to the New Jersey side of the river and watched small turtles as they made their annual migration back to the river. The turtles were going into a hole quite far from the river but we understood that the hole was the entry point to a tunnel that led to the river. We returned to the dorm to pack our luggage since school started the next day and we had to get out. We scurried to pack quickly but before we finished we took a car trip south along the river where we saw our luggage floating in the river (3/10/13).

My dreams seem to occur in cycles. I think I had dreams about ten straight nights in this early March stretch. Last night I dreamed I was working at the construction site for a large new office building. I was cutting down a tree near where my car was parked, and another guy was cutting down a tree nearby. The other guy felled his tree so that it landed perfectly between my car and the tree I was cutting. After I felled my tree I noticed a small breeze coming out of a glass covered box built into the soil. I had seen my father and those of his generation build these boxes, usually with an old storm window laid on top with seedlings planted inside to get an early start on spring. The breeze from a small hole on top of the box blew the sawdust from my tree cutting off the window on top of the box. I looked inside the box and saw many bees scurrying about and on the side wall of the box there were very large spiders about the size of lobsters. I wondered how the spiders, being so large, would be able to get out of the box (3/11/13).

I was at a meet and greet gathering at VFW in my old hometown. When I came out my beloved BMW 3 series was missing. I called my wife who came to pick me up and we drove around looking for it without success (4/1/13).

Attended a political gathering in Bergen County after a big snowstorm. Only the valet area of the parking lot was cleared of snow and there were huge piles of snow all around. I did not want to use valet so I parked down the street partially on top of a snowbank (4/2/13).

Myself, my oldest son and his boss biked (road bikes, not motorcycles) down the East Coast in only 4 days! We were motoring! I forgot my helmet and gloves, so we had to stop on first day to buy new ones (4/3/13).

I was in North Dakota attending a conference when I took a side trip. I was driving through a landscape that was only so-so. I ascended a ridge and on the other side was a gorgeous landscape of hardwood trees in full autumn colors. I was told it was the Mahlon Dickinson Reservation (which is actually in New Jersey)(4/6/13).

I was in my aunt's house which shared a common brick wall with the rug mill in Freehold. The other walls were made of marble which gave the house an exotic look. One wall had a large mural covering the entire wall. The brick wall that was in common with the rug mill had stained glass inserts. It was Christmas Eve and I had yet to put up my Christmas tree. There was an empty bassinet in the house (4/11/13).

I was a vendor at a new auction sales establishment like Englishtown Auction. My twin boys were with me and were wearing hats with signs on them (5/2/13).

Our house was being renovated and we were living in a temporary house. I was in the bathroom admiring a small TV in a corner of the room near the ceiling. I was preparing to shampoo my hair and was surprised that it had grown down to my waist. This was especially surprising since I have been bald for the last 40 years (5/25/13).

At 2:30 in the morning there was a commotion in the front yard of our house in Basking Ridge. Contractors had arrived to demolish an underground one car garage across the street. They couldn't maneuver their construction equipment into position without crossing my front lawn taking down my picket fence and three trees in the process. A friend from town, Babs, showed up and said she could not believe how calm I was with all the destruction that had taken place. I pointed out that the contractor was in violation of Township regulations covering the starting time in the morning for construction and that I was going to report them (6/23/13).

Every so often I have a marathon dream night when I seem to have one dream after another. Such was the case on this night in January 2014 when I awoke to the alarm at 5:30 AM to recall at least five different dreams beginning, I assume, around 12:30 AM. There were two work related dreams which involved being requested to perform traffic studies for a private applicant as well as a town. Another dream involved cleaning out the attic at my parents' house. In another dream I chased stray cats out from under a front porch only to see my own pet cat cross the street and copulate with one of the strays. In my final dream of the night, I was at a garden center patiently waiting as a cashier rung up another customer. When it came my turn the cashier announced the store was closed. I pleaded that I had everything ready to check out and at that point I was awakened by the alarm (1/27/14).

I went to a small airport with Jim, a co-worker, to see a fan-powered flying seat they were about to receive. I had seen one of these advertised on TV at a golf tournament in San Diego. Basically, it consisted of a canvas seat attached to a big fan. We looked at the flying seat but were unsure whether to try it out, it looked too dicey to us. Another guy came along, and he tried it. He got into the seat and turned the fan on and went up about 10 feet above the ground when it flipped over and crashed to the ground with the guy landing on his head. At that point Jim and I agreed a helmet was mandatory if you were going to fly one of these. Jim and I never tried it but Jim's wife, her mother and some guy all squeezed into the seat and took off. They did several inverted loops as the craft careened crazily over a nearby highway. Jim and I thought for sure they were going to crash on the highway but miraculously they landed on their feet on the other side of the highway (1/30/14).

I was living in Morristown NJ when a main trunk sewer line got clogged. I watched as a DPW worker opened a manhole at the bottom of which was a large hole about 40ft. x 60ft. in size. The DPW worker said to me you won't believe how much water will come out of this hole. Water promptly fills the hole and begins to overflow. In the next scene of the dream the entire population of Morristown is in canoes or rowboats floating downstream. I and my family (wife and two kids) are in a Polynesian style canoe with a large engraved bow on the front (3/13/14).

In a second dream of the night, I was still in Morristown at the train station trying to figure out if there was a train to Hightstown. Someone told me there was a train for Postal workers and I should try to catch that (3/4/14).

I was seated at an outside table at a small restaurant in western Virginia on the Maryland border. I was at the table with two other people, one of which was my eldest son. We were told there were a lot of bears in the area but they were pretty tame. As I sat there, the others at the table said a bear was coming up behind me but I should stay calm. The bear put a paw on my right shoulder and proceeded to lick and suck the back of my head. I stayed calm and the bear eventually stopped and went away (3/10/14).

My fathers mom had died. They laid her out in a casket with casters on the bottom at her house. My younger sister was with me, and we were told it was our job to wheel the casket through the streets to the church about ½ mile away. We were about to leave the house when I woke up (3/13/14).

I was delivering furniture while driving a large box truck. One stop was at the parent's house of a part-time employee of our firm. The delivery was a recliner chair for his dad. I spoke to his mom and said I knew her son very well (3/14/14).

I was traveling in a soft world. The streets were hard but lawns and other surfaces had the consistency of marshmallows (3/15/14).

The family was on vacation at a place with a tropical climate. We had an amphibious vehicle that was the size and shape of a large tricycle. We crossed over water and a swamp in this vehicle to reach an isolated cabin in a wooded area on the shore. Later we were swimming in a large lagoon with aquamarine colored water and gentle waves. It was a Disney Park and there were thousands and thousands of people in the water. There were islands in the lagoon with amusement park rides on them. At some point our boys got separated from us but my wife and I seemed unconcerned as everything was tranquil in this "blue lagoon "(3/16/14).

Our house was destroyed by a hurricane, and we went away for a while. We returned to move into a ranch house. There were boxes of clothes and other items all over. Also, one bedroom was still occupied by a man who was due to move out shortly. The dream then switched to our house in Warren County where it seemed the neighbors house on the hill above us was much closer than in real life. Next I am driving in the snow through a beautiful downtown looking for a Christmas Tree. It was snowing so heavily I had to stop the SUV I was driving to clear snow off the windshield and rear window. Then I am driving in the snow down a narrow driveway going slowly behind a couple walking in the driveway. I get back on the road and I look in the rearview mirror to see my two sons and dog in the back of the SUV as well as a Christmas Tree that is crowding them out and forcing them to sit toward outside of the SUV. I proceeded into another dream where there was an oil shortage causing great concern, but it was known that a new pipeline was going to bring oil from Canada to New Jersey. I was driving on the NJ Turnpike and in the wide median there was a pipeline with a giant valve that was being opened by a very large screwdriver that was hanging from a crane. Cars were crawling slowly along the road with their windows open and I started to yell to other drivers that the oil pipeline was being opened and hopefully we would have oil to refuel our cars (5/31/14).

It was raining heavily as my wife and I entered a shoe store. I was wearing slippers, and the right slipper was darker and more worn down than the left. I explained that this was because I wore the right slipper more than the left. I could not find any shoes that fit me so I asked the shoe store salesman if they could just waterproof my slippers instead, which they did, free of charge, no less. My wife brought me a bottle of beer which the shoe salesman grabbed and guzzled it down. When we left the store it had cleared, but despite the blue skies overhead, it was still raining (6/9/14).

Four of us guys were on a long Charity bike ride. We pedaled for miles before stopping. When we started again it began to snow and all but one of us stopped after ½ inch of snow had fallen. We later picked up the one guy with our car when he was trying to cycle up a hill but couldn't gat any traction due to the snow (7/26/14).

I was getting ready to race a horse with my car. The horse was on the left (driver's) side of the car. Just before we were to start the race the horse put his right legs through the car windows – the front leg through the driver's window and the rear leg through the rear driver's side window. It was as if the horse was trying to hold the car back at the start of the race (9/14).

The boys had off school midweek because of the Jewish holidays. We took advantage of it and decided to visit the beach and stay overnight at The Chateau hotel in Spring

Lake. Unfortunately, we had an early northeaster and it was chilly, windy and raining cats and dogs. We all slept late and I started to dream. I dreamt that we were staying upstairs at one of my consulting firm's offices and not at The Chateau. I went downstairs at the office building and found myself in a large atrium with guys in business attire and women in gowns. Although it was only 8 AM I was in the middle of a wedding reception. I saw the bride and tables with snacks on them. Our regional manager was dressed in a white minister's vestment – he had apparently performed the wedding service. I was surprised, as I didn't know he was a minister, and thought maybe it was a power given to him as a municipal engineer. I then noticed the weather was clearing and I went back to my room and the family to tell them we could finally go outside. I then woke up, still in our room at The Chateau, and it was still raining heavily (Sept. 2014).

I was in an altercation with or "had the goods "on some organized crime figures. They found me and ran me down on the street with a "woody" style station wagon. I was so badly injured that paramedics who arrived to assist me said I would not survive and therefore they would inject me with a chemical that would kill me in minutes so I would not suffer. I asked for my wife, and she appeared and held my hand as the paramedics injected the fatal drugs. Minutes went by and nothing happened as I just lay there in the road. I was tempted to wake my wife in bed to tell her if I died while lying in bed it was because of the drug injection. I then realized it was a dream I had, didn't wake her, and fell back asleep (3/8/15).

I was at our family home in early December. My mother was getting out Christmas decorations and placed one in the front window. Then one of my sisters arrived from work. Shortly thereafter the rear doorbell rang, and I went out on the rear porch to investigate but nothing was there. I went back inside and the rear doorbell rang again. I went out to check and again nothing was there. I went back in only to have the rear doorbell ring a third time. I went back out again to check and saw nothing. I went into the backyard and discovered an inflatable plastic dog running around. The dog was very happy and seemed full of mischief. The dog had obviously rang the doorbell. I started to chase him and he was having a grand time avoiding me (8/30/15).

I was riding a motorcycle in the snow with one of my twin sons on the back. He shot an arrow and hit a target. We stopped and he got off the motorcycle and crossed a football goal line as he ran toward the target. He did five quick flips end over end as he ran. He was about ten years old and dressed in a clown costume (November 2015).

I needed a haircut. My hair looked like tree branches. On the left side of my head a "tree branch" extended out about 2 feet before ending in a "T" shape. Other branches extended out from my head as well. I had the T shaped branch cut off below the T and other branches trimmed. I felt like a new man with my trimmed branches (10/19/16).

I was working in Trenton, N.J. in a tall office building for the State of N.J. Our office was working on mapping of river flooding when it became known that the U.S. and Trenton, in particular, was under the threat of a Russian attack. Our office was recruited to help track the Russian attack. High ranking State Officials came up to our office and worked side by side with me to track the attack. To my surprise an old red shed near the base of our building sprouted an enormous cannon. It was getting dark but all the lights in the city remained off. The situation was very tense for about an hour until the threat was thwarted. The lights came back on and everyone celebrated. I saw a member of the U.S. House of Representatives from N.J. on the street below. Many people, including me, made our way to a horse racing track in Trenton to continue the celebration (10/20/16).

For whatever reason I stopped recording dreams in late 2016 and did not record a dream until September 2019 when I had the vivid dream about the white-hot arrow in the sky related at the beginning of this book. Among the more vivid dreams I recall over this three-year period was one where I discovered a nest of yellow jackets under the rear wall at our home in Basking Ridge, a dream involving a flooded basement at my parent's home and finally a dream where I was recruited by the mayor of New Brunswick, N.J. to help with his re-election campaign. I had a strategy meeting with his supporters, all in canoes on a large lake.

I was walking with a friend from high school who was nursing a bad ankle. To lessen the distance, we had to walk we cut a corner across a used car lot. We stopped to look at a wildly colored VW beetle which had large painted rocks in the trunk. Just then a big American car from the 1950's wheeled into the used car lot. The car had about ten dogs in it; one of whom was driving. All dogs were of the same breed – a German Shepard mix with black and grey coloration. The dogs seemed to be on a joy ride (11/15/19).

I was at my parent's house. A trash truck was on the street knocking off lower branches of the large red maple that was in front of the house next to the street. The driver was using the arms that extended out in front of the truck that was used to lift dumpsters to crash into the branches knocking them off. I protested but the driver said the branches had to be removed because they hung over the street and impeded the truck passage down the street (3/20).

I skied at a new ski slope that had just opened in New Jersey. It had only one trail, but the trail was very challenging. It was spring and 84 degrees so I skied wearing shorts (4/4/20).

I dreamt of the week leading up to the opening of the college football season. The first game was to be held at a new stadium built in Washington Township, Warren County. The game was scheduled for Thursday night and on the Tuesday night preceding the game there was an outside basketball game between local stars and another team. One of the teams scheduled to play in the football game was the University of Idaho. To promote the game there were a half dozen mini cars shaped like the state of Idaho driving all over the area. The cars were orange and trimmed in blue (the colors of Boise State) and they would dart in and out of local traffic to promote the game. Two cars were parked perpendicular to the flow of traffic and as every other car passed they would back into the roadway blocking traffic temporarily and then pull forward off the roadway (4/12/20).

I had what seemed to be a reoccurring dream. In these dreams I would leave a friend's house in Basking Ridge by climbing on their kitchen counters and out the kitchen window. I would then walk across a small stream and up a long sloping field to another friend's house about a mile north in Basking Ridge. I would climb in their kitchen window and onto their kitchen counter. I then made the reverse trip going south. Apparently, I was doing this on a regular basis since both couples left their kitchen windows unlocked for me. Why I didn't use doors which were also unlocked in each case is a mystery. I made the trip back to the house in the north when I heard the couple talking out in front of the house. I went out the front door and saw the couple painting by hand an old pickup truck in their driveway. It was green (4/17/20).

I was returning to our house in Warren County with my wife. We had no car and my wife was sitting astride a Holstein cow while I walked alongside holding a leash that was connected to a bridle on the cow. We crossed Route 31 at its intersection with Route 57 and then turned right going up a hill where the street terminated in a dirt trail. We continued going up the hill where the ground was covered by huge boulders the size of cars and larger. It was very difficult and treacherous even for a mountain goat to climb over these boulders – but the cow handled it well. We descended the other side of the hill and saw we were too far to the north of our house so we turned right and ended up walking along the shore of Raritan Bay. The sand was a yellow-orange color and there was a light fog. The cow was no longer with us. The bay was essentially where the Musconetcong Valley is in real life (4/18/20).

I was in Cape May County at a marina complex with a large pier raised about 30 feet above the water. I was negotiating with the marina owner about leasing space at the end of the pier to build a house which would be suspended under the pier opposite an inlet from the ocean. The owner wanted $800 per square inch to lease the space. With me was my cousin (who had died three months earlier in real life) and several other young second cousins from Boston. I demonstrated how cool it would be to live right on the water by taking a door and using it as a paddleboard. My relatives suggested I should check out waterfront properties on peninsulas in Costa Rica (4/22/20).

I was visiting a car dealer just before his 11 PM closing time to look at a new Chevy Impala. I waited ½ hour before they wheeled out an elaborate display on a movable stage which had a car with a full-length mattress that ran from the steering wheel to the back of the car. I told them I didn't want to see any accessories – I just wanted to see the driver's seat and steering wheel. I was not happy and instead of showing interest in the car, I and one of my sons, took a motorcycle for a test drive. I drove with my son on the back and on the return trip he drove with me on the back (4/23/20).

Two short dreams. In first I was a talent agent for a young 7- or 8-year-old boy. I was mostly getting him modeling gigs. I advised him how to dress and behave, etc. In the second dream I was escorting a retired Veteran. I was driving him to an awards ceremony (4/26/20).

Connected dreams interrupted by being awake! My old boss Steve (from the 1970's) was seeking approval from a planning board in NJ to convert a building on a golf course into a residence. A use variance was required and I was representing him. His son was also involved. Neither had prepared for the meeting. We couldn't find the meeting hall which was supposedly located in the northeast corner of the municipality. We did find some municipal offices including the police station as well as a train station and an amusement park. The train station had some amusement park features including fake plastic snowdrifts on the steps. Steve parked his Honda Pilot in a parking garage by going up on a one-way down ramp. Once parked, he covered the car with a gray plastic sheet which matched the color of the car. At this point I woke up. After a while I fell asleep again and dreamt it was the next day. We were attending a Rutgers football game in a brand-new stadium located in the township where Steve was seeking his variance. It had snowed. We met the Planning Board Chairman of this municipality. I introduced him to Steve and his son and mentioned we had missed the Planning Board meeting the night before. As it turns out missing the meeting didn't matter because Steve had failed to get listed on the agenda. The Chairman confirmed the proofs we would need to present to seek approval of the project. The stadium was very industrial looking with lots of gray accented with dark red and mustard colored trim. The game was vs. West Virginia whose players were much bigger than Rutgers and at the half West Virginia led 7 – 0 (4/27/20).

I was visiting a museum in Trenton, N.J. and not for the first time in my dreams. In prior dreams there were very few visitors but this time the museum was very busy. The attendant at the entrance recognized me and said you know your firm has materials in an exhibit here. I said I knew having seen a large pile of rocks in the basement on a previous visit. The rocks were apparently from some sort of drilling operation the firm was doing. I must have been doing research for work because I was calculating the mileage between the museum and my office in order to fill out an expense report (4/28/20).

I purchased a super lightweight sled for my oldest son when he was 12. It was made out of a metal/carbon composite and was all one piece, all of the same material. We brought it to a frozen manmade lake in central N.J. that was specifically designed for ice boats with a long fetch running northwest to southeast to take advantage of the predominant wind direction in the winter. The sled was so light it was easily blown along by the wind, so much so that it was fast enough to outrace a real ice boat that was considered the "yacht" of ice boats. Everyone who saw this was amazed. Afterwards my son and I were toasted at the bar of the very nice clubhouse that overlooked the eastern end of the lake (5/2/20).

I got married as a middle-aged adult. My Mom was in attendance as were other relatives. A cousin from Boston complained that the reception was not up to the standards of a typical Boston wedding (5/4/20).

WORK RELATED

Our office was moving into a new hi-rise building that was still under construction. Stu and Bhim (neither of whom I had seen for 15 years and were not co-workers but professional associates) were co-workers. The final touches were being put to the building as the dream progressed (3/30/10).

I was working with a small group of environmental consultants (some of the staff resembled people I had worked with in the past). They worked out of a small office in someone's house that was on a dead end street with a large pile of dirt stockpiled at end of the street. There was a question as to whether to keep them on the job they were tasked with and whether to hire them as employees or keep them as subconsultants. I consulted with our regional manager and we agreed to keep them on the job as subconsultants (3/31/10).

At the firm I worked at we were putting in long hours on a land use study identifying individual land parcels using a complex procedure. There was a large well attended public hearing on the project which I was scheduled to speak at but at the last minute couldn't attend due to illness. The company President also was scheduled to attend. I called the President on my cell phone to see how the meeting was going and was told my call would be broadcast live into the cafeteria of a school where the meeting was being held. This, of course, made me very nervous. The President was serving as moderator. Afterwards I was told I came across well and posed some good questions (4/1/10).

In my dreams I created a complete use variance application to allow an office on a residentially zoned property. There was a vacant building on the property that the owner wanted to use as an office. He was well-prepared to advance the application at a Zoning Board hearing since he knew the officials and ropes to pull in this well-to-do town. The owner had retained an engineer to testify as well. Just before the hearing was to begin the owner told me that instead of an office, he may rent out the building to a day care center instead. The name of the day care center was the Five Baers. It appeared the hearing was destined not to proceed as there was no Board Attorney present. The Board Attorney finally made an appearance and the meeting started late. There was one application on the agenda before us and as they made their presentation I pondered how I was going to change my testimony from the proofs necessary to support an office application to the proofs I needed to present for a day care center (2/21/12).

I was the expert Planning witness for a Home Depot application. There was an issue related to insufficient parking. My friend was the Planning Board Chair (4/16/13).

A long involved dream that started with me taking a luggage rack off the roof of a VW (interesting in that I never owned a VW like the one in the dream until 6 years after this dream when I owned a Golf Sportwagen with a luggage rack). After removing the rack I saw a hole remained in the roof that required a screw. A co-worker, Jerry, found a screw that would fit in a parts storage compartment that was outside our office in an indentation in a concrete slab. The compartment was filled with water so it was surprising he found the screw. After inserting the screw, I noticed there were other screw holes with cardboard beneath the holes. Before I could tend to them someone reminded me, I was scheduled for a lunch meeting with the director of the Freehold DOT ROW office. I took another co-worker with me and it started to snow; an unexpected snow since it was late spring. Because of the snow we could not make it all the way to the DOT office, and we got out of the car and walked along a snowy wooded slope making a tricky crossing on top of a fallen tree over a chasm. Someone grabbed my arm to help me across. We made it to the office building which was futuristic looking with shops and an arcade on the first floor. The DOT office was on the fourth floor, but we could not find an elevator or stairs. We met some engineers from a foreign country who were also looking for an elevator or stairs. I went to use the mens room and inside came across a narrow door marked ELEVATOR. I went through the door and got onto a swing chair – like the chairs on a rotating swing at an amusement park. There were dozens of these chairs all with people in them. We waited about 5-10 minutes before the chairs began to move and then we were whisked away on a ride through the dark interior of the building going up and down until we were finally deposited on the fourth floor (5/19/13).

Went to a one-day conference in a seaside city. The main presentation I attended was about a new way to market. The presentation was great! At one point I climbed to the top of a grandstand (like those in a gym). The people I was with were very concerned about me climbing to the top for some reason. There was a concluding video that showed happy people cooking a new menu item. One of the people was my co-worker Margaret who had a new hairstyle that was very becoming. She was smiling and looked the best she has in years. On the way out I stopped at a store run by the presenters and discovered that they offered their own brand of shoes with their logo on them. I considered buying a pair but they did not have my size (5/26/13).

I was at a Special Planning Board meeting at a township in Morris County. There was a canal in the township that passed through the center of the meeting room. It was a Friday night before a holiday weekend, and everybody was surprised that a special meeting was called for this night. We heard that the reason was the applicant had a new planner who was only available on this night. The court reporter who was there to transcribe the meeting was apparently too warm as she took her blouse off and sat there only with her bra on her upper body. The court reporter suddenly left the room and was gone for a long time. Other females present reported that she was vomiting in the ladies room. Eventually she returned to the meeting room but the meeting had not yet started. There had been a lot of rain and after the meeting had started the canal, which was contained in a concrete channel, overflowed onto the meeting room floor and we were soon up to our knees in water. The meeting was adjourned and I walked down the road a short distance to retrieve my camper trailer parked in the campground which was now full of weekenders (10/1/13).

I was out of the office for a week on vacation when I became aware of a new NJDOT project that the firm had a contract for and after reading the project scope of work it became apparent that it was the type of job that "was right up my alley ". It involved a corridor study for Route U.S. 206 in Burlington County that included evaluations of land uses and possible condemnation. I started work on it and was looking forward to spending more hours on the project when I was told the CEO of our firm did not want me to work on it. This was puzzling since of all the people in the firm I was the most qualified to work on this type of study. I could only conclude that it was a signal from the CEO that I should think about retirement (1/20/14).

I went back to the office well after hours to retrieve something and to turn a detector of some sort off that I had mistakenly left on (1/21/14).

I was at work in the field helping a supervisor scout out the canoeing possibilities on a stream. We had prepared a planning study that proposed a new community along this stream and stated that one of the amenities could be a canoe livery on the banks of the stream. So me and my supervisor were riding up and down the stream on a road that was on the banks of the stream to see if the stream was suitable for canoeing. I had a small ultralight canoe attached to the side of my car in the event I wanted to sample the current (2/1/14).

I was being interviewed, along with other consultants, to prepare a site suitability study for a hotel on a small lot in a residential area close to a light rail station. The person who was hired had to convince the public that it was a suitable site for the hotel. During a break in the interview process I took a ride on the light rail out and back several stops and past the hotel site to see how accessible the site was. The light rail cars had no roofs and were open to the sky. The seating was bleacher style with each row of seats rising above the one in front of it. This seating seemed dangerous. I had to make one transfer which made it difficult to get back to the interview on time (3/14/14).

This is a weird one. The dream was in October 2015, but I did not record it in my journal until 4 years later. It was so vivid that I remembered most of the details four years later. My boss was giving me my annual performance review. He was wearing a helmet-like mask. More significantly, he had a nose mole. This was a small mole-like creature that lived in a human's nose and kept it clear of nose debris (boogers). As my boss spoke to me his nose mole kept poking his head out of the boss's nostril. It was very distracting. My boss asked me if I still wanted to be "a member of the club" which I took to mean continue to be an employee (10/15).

I retired from my company in September 2018 but the work related dreams did not. Frequently the dreams had a deadline which was impossible to meet. I was the manager at a branch office and had to arrange a brief entertainment for the staff at lunchtime. Someone told me of a small marching band and I arranged for a dry run of the band for me and the firm's coordinator of entertainment whose approval I needed. The band marched through the office after hours and the entertainment coordinator loved it. I told her I thought maybe it was too much with flailing arms and legs and crashing cymbals, but she said no – it was good (11/23/19).

We are in the midst of the Covid pandemic and have been ordered to stay in place for two weeks by the Governor. My twin boys have come home from college and are taking classes remotely. My wife is also home working remotely. The real world is topsy-turvy, but my dream world remains intact. I have at least one dream per night but more typically I have two or three that I recall when I awaken. For some reason just about all my dreams for a two-month period were work related.

I had been called out of retirement to meet with a group of developers in Millburn, N.J. My former company's president was with me and we were meeting with the developers in their office which was on the second floor of a building that was heavily damaged by fire. All the doors were closed and inoperative, so we had to climb through windows to get in which, as it turns out was quite difficult, especially given our advanced age. We had to contort our bodies and pull ourselves up with our arms through the windows which were hinged at the top and swung outward and up. On the inside there was little room to place our feet as glass shelves lined the walls under the windows. The developer guys were much better at climbing through the windows, even though some were my age. They were gung-ho about their work and not easily deterred (4/6/20).

I caught a bus to Paterson, N.J. with several co-workers. I spoke to the bus driver who was a big genial guy who I really related to. It turns out he was from my hometown. At the end of our bus trip there were several bus drivers hanging out. I Asked if any had read White Widow – a novel about a bus driver written by Jim Lehrer. Only one driver said he had, but that he couldn't relate to it. The purpose of our trip to Paterson was to meet with a group opposed to the extension of I-85 through their city. They were interested in us doing a report to oppose the highway construction. We visited the site of the proposed extension only to find that an area a block wide had been cleared of buildings and piers were already in place to support an elevated roadway. At that point we advised the group it was too late to retain us to prepare a report objecting to the location of the highway (4/7 20).

I was in Georgia with a consulting team we had formed including my best friend and another guy. We were interviewing to prepare a plan for a new town in Florida being proposed by a private developer. At the interview there were four consulting teams. Each team was eventually awarded part of the contract. As we left the interview everyone on each of the consultant teams was given a bag which contained two pastries and an 8 x 10 color photo of themselves that was taken when they entered the interview room. On the photo words were inscribed describing the individual's clothing and an interpretation of their bearing/gravitas. I was wearing a tan suit with a brightly colored tie that was aqua and beige, plus tan loafers. The words describing my appearance included the supposed designer name of the suit and my posture. As I left the interview room I asked what part of the contract we were awarded and I was told produce and Alaska (4/17/20).

I was at work preparing for a noon meeting which was called to review and critique a report prepared by others. It was 11:35 AM. As I reviewed the report, I realized the time had advanced to 11:55 AM and I wasn't ready. I started to get out of bed with the thought that I needed to at least put on a pair of pants for the meeting. As I swung my left leg out of bed I awoke. I sat on the bed dazed for a few minutes before I realized I was dreaming (4/23/20).

It is May 9th – the coldest May 9th on record in my part of NJ. The low was 30 and the high 46. I mowed the lawn in snow showers that afternoon. In upstate NY they had 12in. of snow and 15 inches in Maine. My dream that night was work related as I was testifying before a municipal Planning Board. When I left the meeting, I realized I had not driven my car to the meeting. I went outside and asked a young mother if I could borrow her station wagon. She complied and took her toddler out of the back seat and I drove her car to my home in the snow. I returned it the next day.

The work-related dreams are too numerous to describe each in detail. Here is a summary of several dreams beginning on May 10, 2020:

Came across a pad site in a mall in Ocean County that was occupied by an office of National Home Mortgage

Finance Agency. I told a representative of this organization I was a Planner and could locate additional sites for them to expand, but approvals might be difficult. I then produced my business card and said I could testify for any approvals (5/10/20). I had abdominal surgery and I was released from the hospital the next day and met with a group of about 20 experienced consultants in planning and environmental matters, all of whom, including me, had joined together to start a new firm. We discussed what type of work we would pursue and how to approach proposal writing (5/29/20). I was approached by NJDOT to prepare a proposal to either remove or screen with vegetation a battleship that was in a detention basin at NJDOT headquarters (5/30/20). I was retained as a consultant to object to a school tax increase in Point Pleasant. I dug up a plant from a marsh to use as a prop at the hearing but didn't get reached and had to dispose of the plant in a trash can inside the community building since the box I put it in had begun to fall apart from moisture from the plant (5/31/20). I was working as a Planner for a NJ Township where the number of units in a proposed multi-family development was to be determined by the size of a cake baked or brought in by the proposed developer. A frequent applicant in the Township brought in a cake shaped like a pumpkin and I took a photo of it. The night of the hearing an objector complained the number of units proposed was not supported by the size of the cake. I went to retrieve the cake, but it had been half eaten by municipal employees and the remainder was in the trash. I tried to estimate the original size of the cake based on my photo and what I had retrieved from the trash waking up as I did so (5/6/21). My former consulting firm had built a new ultra-modern office building in the shape of an egg of which they were the sole occupant. We took a tour of the new building. My wife was now an employee and had a reserved nook. I wondered if there was a reserved space for me as a retired employee. Upon leaving the sidewalk was very icy from freezing rain. I got a running start and flopped onto my belly and slid what seemed like forever down the sidewalk all while wearing a three-piece suit (11/26/21).

BACK TO THIS AN THAT

Dreams other than work related dreams occur on nearly a nightly basis. On June 15,2020 I had a night full of pleasant dreams. They included a fun-filled cattle drive and then a golf match. Then after 7:30 AM I dreamt I was in a hardware store buying a spark plug for my lawnmower. I knew the spark plug had a number of nine thousand and change but the store had a number of plugs with numbers like 9117w. So, I purchased two plugs with different numbers plus I also purchased a windbreaker. I then walked across a courtyard and purchased something in another store. I opened the bag from the hardware store to put the newly purchased item in it and the sales girl reached into the bag and pulled out a fleece baby's outfit with a hood. I had no idea how it got into my bag. The salesgirl said the outfit would be great for the beaches on the Cape. I said she must be a Gleason and she said no, but her best friend was named Gleason and she brought me to her friend who was conveniently seated in an adjoining room. I said I knew Ms. Gleason through her father and pointed to him as he was seated next to her. The father was an attorney who I had worked with. This dream came a day after we had signed a lease to rent a condo in Cape May from a person named Gleason.

I dream just about every night but do not always record them. Some nights I have several that stand out. Like this one where I was in a race with four teams, each team having two people. There were four means of racing: using a Go-cart; hopping in a large football-type helmet placed on our feet; plus, two other means. My team was winning - lapping the other teams after two circuits around a track hopping in our helmets. A second dream this night involved helping my mom plan improvements to her house. Contractors had opened a trench exposing all utilities from the street into the house. I could see into the basement by standing in the trench and observed there were no leaks. My last dream of the night was very vivid. Greg Schiano (Rutgers football coach) was a deal closer at a car dealership in Budd Lake NJ. I had done something to upset other members of the sales team who were mafia types. They were chasing me around the dealership brandishing handguns when Greg came to my rescue and said he was a friend of mine (9/7/20).

Greg Schiano appeared in another of my dreams a little over a year later. I was at a Red Sox game, possibly a World Series game, but not at Fenway. I was on the field down the right field line in foul territory when a hard-hit ball whizzed past me and hit the outfield wall. It bounced off the wall and back toward me. I retrieved it and put it in the left front pocket of my madras patterned Bermuda shorts. I later took the ball out and discovered it had a dent where the bat had hit it. I then went to the area of the bullpen, which was for some reason, behind the homeplate stands. The pitcher's mound was in a reservoir of water. A pitcher, who looked like Roger Clemens, walked off the mound into the water while wearing a felt fedora. He became completely submerged and continued to walk away from the mound, on the bottom of the reservoir finally returning to the mound after apparently demonstrating how long he could hold his breath. Next, I found myself standing in the concourse area behind homeplate. In front of me was Greg Schiano. A guy standing to my left reached out and placed a note in Greg's rear pants pocket. Greg whirled around to see who had done this and I pointed to my left. Greg said "you again, you have been following me all over". The guy explained he was a doctor from Los Angeles, and he was giving Greg notes on a holistic diet he thought Greg should follow. I got Greg's attention and said I was a Rutgers football fan and asked what player on the team had the most potential to develop into a star player. Without hesitation Greg said Chris Daniels (12/9/21).

I was on the 16th floor of a high-rise building with another male and two females. We had to get the ground without passing through the building because our enemies were on the staircases and in the elevators. So we made a rope out of shirts and pants tied together and descended one by one hand over hand. The scariest part was there was an overhang on our floor that extended out about 20 feet so that when each person went over the edge those remaining above could not see them until they reached the ground and signaled they were OK (9/22/20).

I was touring Europe visiting England and France. In France I took a trip up what was advertised as Europe's tallest mountain. Up until about 1,000 feet from the summit it wasn't steep and there was a road ascending the mountain with housing along the road as if it wasn't a mountain at all. But near the top the mountain became exceptionally steep and the only way to access the top was by climbing into a small roller coaster type vehicle. Each car was so small that backpacks were not allowed, and it was a tight fit for me. There were no restraining straps or bars, only a bar on each side of the car to hold onto. The ascent was so steep it averaged 90 degrees and at one point the track bent backwards beyond 90 degrees vertical so that if you didn't hang on you would have fallen out! This was very scary (9/23/20

Dream Along With Me

Dreamed about an old neighbor who was two years younger than me but had gone astray with drugs after high school and after I had gone away to college. I think I only saw him once or twice after high school. In the dream he apparently had reformed and become a High School Resource Officer. He was wearing a N J State Trooper uniform with the words Resource Officer embroidered across the shoulders. He was giving a presentation at a high school, and he came down from the stage to greet me as I was sitting in the front row. I got his address on a slip of paper so that we could get together but lost it as the dream ended. Later the same night I had a second dream where I came across the missing slip of paper with an address in Berkeley Heights N J. I awoke and realized this friend had died about 8 years earlier so there was to be no getting together (10/8/20).

Despite no relevant experience I was recruited to take over as the director of a psychiatric unit at a mental hospital in Connecticut. I traveled there and was offered the job, which I accepted, coming out of retirement to do so. The outgoing director was burned out and needed to retire himself. I was told my most daunting task was to keep tabs on Mr. Davy Green, an ex-athlete from East Orange, N.J. Mr. Green was free to come and go as he pleased but had a propensity to give money to anyone with a good story about their need for money. He was a good guy willing to share the fortune he had made as an athlete but would surely go broke if he wasn't watched carefully (12/2/20).

Two vivid dreams in one night. In my first dream my wife's younger sister was married to Bruce Springsteen. My wife and I accompanied the Springsteens to several dinners that were held in firehouse/VFW hall type settings. One dinner was somewhere in the Carolinas with about 150-200 people in attendance. I stood up and introduced Bruce, his wife and my wife noting that I was married to Bruce's wife's sister. The next two gatherings were in Brick and Neptune City, N.J. with much smaller crowds and again I introduced everyone and noted our relationship (1/13/21).

In my second dream I was traveling with my boss on a business trip. I had to stop and visit a Home Depot explaining to my boss that I needed something but couldn't recall what it was. I planned to walk up and down the aisles of the store to jog my memory and told my boss it would only take a few minutes. I did find three items but dropped the receipt. A store manager and I proceeded to look for the receipt, wasting much time. I looked at my watch and saw I had been in the store over ½ hour. I tried to call my boss on my cell phone to apologize and woke up while dialing (1/13/21).

I am walking about a mile from my house on Washburn Avenue with a wooded area on my right. Suddenly a panther is running toward me but off to the side. He is lean and very fast and fluid, almost gliding through the woods. But he pays me no heed as he runs past me passing within 50 feet of me. Then another panther of the same size follows quickly along the same path followed soon after by three slightly smaller panthers. All 5 panthers were lean and very fast and of a medium gray color, not black. After the last panther passed, I became aware of something moving by my waist on my right. I lashed out with my right arm which landed on the bed with a thump waking me up (1/14/21).

I visited a firm where I was shown a candle that when lit emitted smoke in the shape of stars with individual's birthdates on them. A second dream involved my widowed mother-in-law getting married a second time with the reception at a Burger King. Burger King was running a special on hosting wedding receptions. Afterwards, guests attended a large waterpark on the banks of a lake (3/31/21).

I was wearing a pair of shoes designed for sliding – not the first time I have dreamed of wearing sliding shoes. The shoes performed similar to skis and in prior dreams I was able to slide for miles. In my current dream a friend recruited me to a sliding shoes training school where we could learn tricks, etc. I was much older than most students but had very good sliding shoes which turned out to be the gray Crocs that I wore around the house. The dream was so realistic I "Googled" sliding shoes the next day. The most common definition was shoes that slid on easily followed by roller skates. The closest approximation was newly released tennis shoes developed by Wilson Sports with "glide plates" in the soles so that one doesn't stop abruptly on the tennis court. According to an Ad the shoes "provide the right amount of slide" (4/3/21).

I actually had a night in the first week of April where I had no dream I could recollect. Unusual for me. On some nights I dream what seems to be just about the entire night. This night was one of those. My wife and I went to dinner and upon leaving, before taking my car from the valet, the owner of the restaurant subjected me to a sobriety test. He was doing this to every driver before they got into their vehicle. As I waited for my car I had a gin & tonic in my hand which I gulped down as much as I could before spilling the rest on the ground. Fortunately, I passed the sobriety test. My wife and I then went to an outdoors show set on two hillsides separated by a deep valley. The performers, who were doing a reenactment of biblical times with live cattle as part of the set, were in the valley and the audience was seated on one of the hillsides. Suddenly a famished looking lion bounded down the hillside opposite the audience and attacked the cattle. The performers and audience sought shelter in a nearby building. My wife and I left and next were at an airport where there was some sort of emergency. I was asked by airport authorities to fly a two engined passenger plane out of harms way even though I had never flown a plane before. I took the controls and flew the plane from one end of the airport to the other flying sideways at one point to fit the wings between two buildings. My wife reported that I did a good job and the airport manager, who was also a talent agent, thought I had the makings of acting in a movie. He wanted me to change my looks so that I would have a shaved head, mutton chops and tattoos on my arms. While at the airport I observed several guys running down the runway with wings folded behind their backs. When they reached the appropriate speed, they unfolded their wings and began to fly. I, of course, wanted to try this but was concerned I couldn't run fast enough to take off. The airport management said they gave anyone who wanted to fly a fitness test before letting them attempt flying. I agreed to the test. They gave me an instrument that had a tube with a dial and wires that connected to clips for my ear lobes and one big toe. By breathing into the tube, they were able to tell if I had the lung capacity to run fast enough to take off. I failed the test. I asked how close I was to passing in percentage terms and one guy said I did pretty good for a 50-year-old. I informed them I was 74 and awoke realizing I had become too old to fly (4/10/21).

I was the engineer on a train but the train was not on tracks but on the streets of a downtown. My son was following the train in a car and signaled that I should turn left. To do so I had to back the train up so that I would have enough room to make a wide turn. I made a wide sweeping left turn without mounting the curb on either side of the street (10/3/21).

I was in a long narrow room with caskets piled on top of each other. It was during the Covid 19 pandemic and there were not enough workers in funeral homes or cemeteries to bury the dead so caskets with bodies in them were piling up. At the end of the pile of caskets a woman motioned me to join her. She then opened a casket and pulled out a body. The body had been that of a normal sized man, but it had shriveled up into an inverted cone. When the woman picked the body up its mouth opened and the head turned, and the eyes opened. The woman explained this was a normal reflex reaction that happened even in cadavers that had been dead for some time (12/11/21).

A guy with an actual parrot head was running for mayor and I was one of his supporters. We fondly called him "parrot head "(1/3/22).

I was on a large waterslide. Actually, it was like a small mountain with water flowing down the side. To get to the top there was a conveyor system with locks similar to a canal that mechanically moved up the side of the mountain. The locks were oriented in a horizontal fashion, and each contained water with prople inside. The locks discharged the people at the top who then surfed or body-surfed down the part of the mountain with free-flowing cascading water. It was quite the rush (1/3/22).

I had a series of dreams that were more like a series of scenes:

- Playing goalie on a soccer team with only four players per team and the other three members of my team were teenagers but I was middle-aged.

- I wanted to vote. I was told I had to vote at the Brobek Norsemen office in Fort Dix. Not the first time I have had this dream of being told to vote at the Brobek Norsemen office.

- At a conference. After the morning session, we were told to pick-up sub style sandwiches on our way out. Not everyone did, however, which caused my boss, who was an organizer of the conference, concern about the leftovers.

- I was back at the conference and acting as an escort for someone from Nigeria. I told him to pick up a sandwich on the way out. But he exited before me and failed to pick up a sandwich. Later, my boss stopped by and asked how come the Nigerian did not pick-up his sandwich.

- Back to the soccer game. Someone placed a baseball hat and varsity jacket (with leather sleeves) in the aluminum stands at the field. The hat had about a dozen yellow jackets in it and they were building a nest. The hat was upside down on top of the jacket. I folded the jacket up around the hat and crushed it with my hands and then my knees. I could hear the yellow jacket bodies crunching as I applied more and more pressure. I thought I had killed them all but when I returned later one yellow jacket was still flying around the varsity jacket (1/9/22).

I was in the Army in Vietnam. Everybody was constantly taking showers to keep cool and to wash the sweat away. I was discharged and vowed that I would chronicle the lives of those I served with (1/24/22).

I had many long rambling dreams in early 2022 which I have chosen not to relate here because they were so lengthy and not particularly interesting. A short one that I would like to relate is one where I was snow skiing with a friend and we decided it would be a good idea to put honey on the bottom of our socks so that our feet would stick better to the boots with the added benefit of making our feet smell better (5/4/22).

Dreamt a family friend Lauren was picking up my daughter at my parent's house in a 5-liter yellow Mustang convertible. Lauren was revving the engine which had a deep guttural roar. I believe I had a dream several years ago where Lauren was driving a different 5-liter Mustang. This dream is interesting on several counts. My daughter never lived at my parent's house and Lauren is a very environmentally conscious individual who would more likely be driving a Prius and not a hot Mustang (5/11/22).

I was trying to escape from a communist country. Freedom was on the other side of a used car lot operated by a communist official who monitored the lot to make sure no one crossed to freedom. The lot became empty after all the cars were sold and for some reason the operator became distracted enabling me and my wife to walk across the lot to freedom (5/18/22).

We moved to a new house in late August, and I had several surgeries which resulted in either a lack of dreams or no interest in recording them. However, I can report that my first dream involving the new house had me leaving via the side door with my wife right behind me. As I opened the door I became aware of four wolves waiting outside the door. One managed to wedge himself through the partially opened door and I screamed – waking myself as well as my wife from a sound sleep (12/7/22).

I was shopping in the produce section of a supermarket when I came across my wife's niece's husband who lives about 5 miles from us. He was taking all the peaches and left with three large potato sacks full of peaches. Only about a dozen peaches, all of them in poor condition, remained. Another customer comes in to the produce section, sees all the peaches are gone, and says I see Mike has been here (12/8/22).

I attended a birthday party hosted by my parents for one of their grandchildren. Their house was a house I had never been to. Two of my sisters were there but my oldest sister was running late. A man in a Good Humor truck arrived to deliver ice cream. The ice cream was not in containers but instead was in the form of large slabs about 2 ft. long and 1 ½ ft. wide. He delivered cherry vanilla and chocolate with nuts. He put back into the truck a slab of vanilla chocolate chip explaining that it was inferior because it was artificially flavored and since this flavor was my oldest sister's husbands favorite, he didn't want to disappoint him. He said he would go back to the factory and return with naturally flavored pure ice cream. We didn't tell him that my oldest sisters husband had passed away years ago. My parents then revealed that my oldest sister was planning to buy a former Bell Telephone switching station and convert it into a house. These buildings were made of brick and very sturdy but were only about 20ft. by 20ft. and one story. The building was close by so we set out to visit it (1/26/24).

I was at a Rutgers football rally. We were on the New Brunswick side of the Raritan River when it was announced a bus was available to take us across the river to the stadium. It turned out it was a floating bus and to enter it you had to dive under water and enter the bus through a membrane hole in the floor of the bus. I opted to enter feet first which meant my head was under water much longer as others in the bus pulled me into the bus by my ankles (2/10/24).

One of my most vivid and lengthy dreams ever found me going to Prague as part of a cultural exchange program. I had never been there, so before leaving I asked several people who had, what it was like. All had the same response, saying it was muddy. When I arrived, I found it was true – mud was everywhere. Outdoor statues in public parks all had mud around them and mud was splashed on the lower portions of the statues. I was paired with a young father who had a new dog who wouldn't eat. He asked me what I fed my dog and as I started to tell him I was ushered into a car with two women. As we sat in the car waiting for whatever was to come next an employee from a nearby McDonald's came to the car with small pastry treats which she handed us through the open windows of the car. We then visited a number of small souvenir shops, some with museum quality artifacts. Several of the patrons of these shops had visible deformities. There were two older men, one of whom had a crooked back and was bent over at what seemed an impossible angle. The other man had oversize legs like tree trunks that widened out at the bottom but instead of feet his legs were pointed at the bottom. A third gentleman was pouring a beer out of a jagged broken glass into his right eye socket (there was no eyeball) and swallowing the beer through his eye socket. It wasn't clear to me whether these deformed individuals were actual patrons or props hired by the shops to draw the interest of tourists.

The dream continued as I was joined by my wife and one of my sons and we got into a smaller vehicle similar to a Ford Bronco II. I drove the vehicle up a walkway on a hill filled with pedestrians. When they complained I explained my son had a disability and couldn't walk up the hill. After ascending to the top of the hill we descended on the other side while still in the vehicle. The descent was very long and steep. We gained speed as we descended, and I couldn't slow down. At one point it felt as if the road fell away beneath us and we had the feeling of being weightless. The vehicle kept accelerating and architectural elements such as building columns flew past us in the air similar to stars rushing past a spaceship. It was like being on a runaway roller coaster only faster and was very exhilarating if not downright scary. This is how my visit to Prague ended (3/28/24).

www.ingramcontent.com/pod-product-compliance
Lightning Source LLC
LaVergne TN
LVHW011730060526
838200LV00051B/3105